wine**and**cheese

wine**and**cheese

Justin Cheeseman

...for the ones that I hold close
I love and miss you Granny

contents

acknowledgement   **ix**
preface   **xi**

Justin

"Gentle Giant"   19
"Lies"   31
"Intuition"   37

Alexander

"Love Is"   45
"Devil In A Blue Dress"   71
"Pain"   75

Cheeseman

"Anything"   93
"Adequate"   97

acknowledgement

This book would have not been possible without the unconditional support from a great number of people.

I have to start by thanking my parents Lee and Cedessia. They have always supported me in any endeavors I chose to pursue and words cannot quantify the amount of love I will always have for them. I finally realize how lucky I am to have them in my life, and I absolutely could not imagine this book being realized without them.

I want to also express my gratitude towards my editor, Tahara and the BlackGold Publishing team. When thinking about publishing a book I had no real foundation or map on how to start this process. I found out that Tahara had started a publishing company and realized that this book could finally be a reality for me. They don't realize how thankful I am for them taking on the publishing of my first book. I am forever grateful of them for taking the time to work with me on this project.

I extend a special thanks to Tori who provided the cover work for my book. She has been able to take what I was imagining and bring it to life on paper. Thank you for dedicating your time to help me.

My final thanks goes to you. The one who took the time to read my book. Words cannot express what it means for you to take that chance to read my poetry. I hope in reading this you were able to find some helping words or maybe even saving grace.

Thank you

preface

wineandcheese

is a short collection of poems and
quotes dealing with Love,
Happiness, Loneliness, People,
Inspiration, and Servitude.

this is it.

Justin

Don't take your own life

It just passes the pain

To all the ones who know your name

Keep to yourself
Don't let anyone in
Not every smile
deserves to be your friend

Are the gates shut tight?

Been sealed for years

You hear someone knocking…

you open up the gate to let them in

Just to absorb all their sin

Keep your stones

closetoyou

Dig one ditch

You better dig two

A lie is around the

world

While the truth is

still putting its shoes on

Hope has killed more dreams

than faith ever will

Wondering in the dead of night

Looking through the wall

Would it even matter if I call

The leaves gone with the wind

Are
they
just
following
the latest trend?

Combating their sad lives by giving in

or maybe they know it will begin again

As the darkness crept in

I put forth my hand

to guide you to the light

Walking
alone
down
the
pale
road

Seeing figures

pass me by

Never
wanting
to
say
goodbye

I can't get out, I need a helping hand

I keep clawing but all I grab is sand

You can't save them all

Is what I was told

But I'll be damned

If I'm ever that cold

Always be kind

From day

to day

You might save a life

In the most peculiar way

When your dreams turn to nightmares

Your world will be besieged

Be patient time will give you reprieve

If you confide in them
Yet they never follow up
Don't believe they care
Everyone has time
if they want to be there

Stop wishing for better days

Go
get your dreams

before you are stuck

playing for the other teams

Tall and quiet
Like a Sequoia tree
Absorbing all the pain for free
This tree won't fall, this tree won't sway
It
will
always
be here to stay

You trying to
make them
happy

but you aren't
happy

A dark passenger

Sitting in the rearview

Waiting on you to miss your curfew

I must live alone

Patiently waiting for one to take the

throne

Knowing the winter

Is my *realest* fear

Waiting to claim me

Not just once a year

The one you love

Should you just... let go?

Always
wondering
s o you'll never grow

He looks down

on the others

because they are weak

Fighting every day

for the driver seat

Kicking and screaming

As it dragged them out the house

Their father already left,

He was just a shell

No one could save the innocent

From this living hell

I took the step to heal you
while you walked out the door

Let go of the sorrow

It won't last forever

You control your life

Embrace the weather

Death comes quick

It can't be late to class

Abandon your pride

No need to be crass

When you trust someone

Be wary letting them in

They will lie to you with a

Not a fort

nor a strong*hold*

No place in my *mind*

where I have a *foothold*

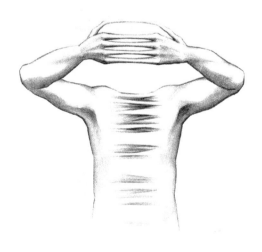

Don't change up

For the ones who have been there

through thick and thin

You will want them back

after you don't win

You have never seen me?

I'm   always   hidden

Trapped

in a

complex

maze

Every

pathway

explored

Places

me   closer

to his

gaze

Fighting through the trenches

Always
in
a
constant struggle

There is no light

When no one knows you're in trouble

You only know
what I *want* you to know
No human is ready
for the full scope of this show

I wonder when you are feeling great
Feeding you information from my plate.

Hurt the ones that care

Play the victim every part

Revenge is nothing

Once retribution wants it start

It's
Cold

Winter has come to stay

**No love
can be found here**

Spring will never be on its way

Cry softly
my dear

Your sorrows will eventually clear

If you have to demand
better treatment
You have already lost
yourself
Take a step back
Recognize
your wealth

No mistakes were made

Just lessons learned

Alexander

Long days
Long nights

Living everyday with no end in sight
Always trying to do what's right
She just wants a copilot on her flight.

Love is like a planet
Rotating around the sun
Hoping this star is the one

I'd rather you
just say no

Don't go around
kissing cotton
Even the ones that look soft
can be rotten

A whistling girl and a crowing hen
Never come to a good end
Always fly my friend

Scat cat let me see your kittens

I yearn
for her taste

Every woman has left her mark
imprinted on me forever

The shallow gasp
the squirming of her hips
Is what I live for

All I needed was her smile
everything else was extra

You needed me
until you found another

You hadn't had sex
You were busy making love

Its fine
Just don't lie

When you try
to break down the walls to help
Just to find out
they never intended to be there

When we first met
she said I didn't have a chance
I fell into love
and she had me in her trance

Beckon for the truth
Honesty is key
The liar will be easy to see

Be direct and forthcoming
Jump at the chance
Many people have died
So you wouldn't save the last dance

She always had this look
That made me unfold
I loved my best friend
but I never told

Innocence is never lost
Your heart just realized
How much it cost

Why lie to me?

I was always close
You lost someone who cared the most

Open the window
She yelled from her keep
Not realizing she was asleep

Drinking with the devil
Is one hell of a game
Trying to bargain
Through all the shame

The knot in your chest
Feels like a ton
Hoping it disappears
Before you meet your son

Love is a splendid disaster
Filled with sadness and laughter

Hold them close my dear

Death doesn't waiver
when the time is near

God won't protect you
She will watch you fall
only coming to your need

if you crawl

You let me go
Without a second thought
Casting me out to watch me rot

Why did you try
When you weren't ready

She approached me with a smile

Her lies ran further than the Nile
I silently thought she was no good
I should back out now while I could
it was too late, I fell into her depression
Thinking I was the priest,
accepting her confession
I was not ready for her pain
She used me up for her personal gain

Be happy it graced you with its touch
Love is a beast
but can't be tamed as such

It will sweep you off your feet
While have you crying in your seat
Open your heart for that chance again
Love will come back as your old friend

I didn't want to love you
Then I took the chance
I fell in love with your words
Entranced by their dance
You said you love me
with all your heart
Just to leave me torn apart

What I didn't realize
Was she was broken
Fighting to figure out love
I decided to see if I could repair her
Until I realized
that is not how love works

Despite my hardest attempts
to show her I was there
All of my breaths fell on thin air

Now I see how detrimental love can be
She chose another
after she said she said she loved me

I'll always cherish the memories we had
Those small moments in time
warm my soul
I finally realized
how beautiful love can be

It rocks you to the core
Waiting for you
not to stand up anymore
Tearing into your life
Filling it with angst and strife

Its ok to cry
its ok to feel
That just lets you know it's real

All I see is misery
As they hang from the tree
Pale faces staring deep
Ensuring I get no sleep

Cheeseman

I hope I win the lottery

but I didn't
buy any

tickets

Sometimes you have to
burn one to light one

Catch the first thing smoking
Don't let the dust settle

Worried about the dollar
when you don't have fifty cents

During the coldest nights

I wonder if God really does exist

or if she sees
how much I care about her children

Always tired
hoping for a better day
I get plenty of sleep
It just doesn't go away
Sitting in the corner
Staring me down
I hate when it comes around

Cornered by the others here
Trying to smile through the fear

One says this
one says that

Only the silent one has my back

Incapable to grasp
Impossible to learn
One day you'll have your turn

Don't abandon
the ones that have held you down
You'll wake up one day and realize
everybody has left your town

Neurons firing off in quick succession
Trying to slow one for a little protection
No way I can stop their pace

They are all running
but don't have a race

You needed them
They didn't need you
Life won't always give you a clue

Sometimes you have to
Light the kettle on fire

The mist settled slowly
As I set on the porch
In the distance an entity walked closer
All it had was a torch
I stood up quick to give it a greeting
But it stated it was here for a meeting
Curious, I said "With who?"
It responded all three of you

To young to know what it really meant
Her mother was only
trying to find a gent
Many men in and out the door
She wanted to find love
by opening her store
So anyone could just stroll in
Taking all of her secrets
she keeps within

Keep it secret
Quite as a mouse
Until the cat comes
To burn down the house

Waiting to claim me
Not just once a year
Keeping my happiness
Far from near
It doesn't last forever
So there is always cheer

The one who was created
when they split
He keeps us safe, but never quit
The one that comes out
when we've been done wrong
No one knows his silent song

You let your failure control you?
Sins of your past
working hard to hold you?

Break free of that grief
Steal your happiness like a thief

Will you always be second
never good enough
Trying to play from the rough
or will you be first
Ready to jump on board
leading your life
from the tip of the sword

If you have to tailor your actions
to fit their mold

the relationship won't last
When everything is told

It feels good
to let your soul out on a stroll
Journey to a new place
Without paying the toll

Always seen the best in people
No matter the case
Even if they showed me the worse,
straight to my face
Always thinking they would do no harm
Instead I was fooled

by their devilish charm

I hate liars, I'll never lie to you
Only to find you were never true
While you chose to lie to my face
I always kept you in the highest place

I just lost my hands
They cut off my hands
Without a fleeting thought
They let me bleed out on the cot

Let out all your pain
Rejoice in your tribulations

One takes control
the others silently wait
Pondering if anyone will catch this trait
All of them want to be free
While all of them can't be me

CPSIA information can be obtained
at www.ICGtesting.com
Printed in the USA
LVHW081724270319
612041LV00018B/323/P